More

MATH
PUZZLES AND PATTERNS
FOR KIDS

T0314600

KRISTY FULTON

Routledge
Taylor & Francis Group

NEW YORK AND LONDON

First published in 2008 by Prufrock Press Inc.

Published in 2021 by Routledge
605 Third Avenue, New York, NY 10017
2 Park Square, Milton Park, Abingdon, Oxon OX14 4RN

Routledge is an imprint of the Taylor & Francis Group, an informa business

Copyright © 2008 Taylor & Francis Group

Production Design by Marjorie Parker

All rights reserved. No part of this book may be reprinted or reproduced or utilised in any form
or by any electronic, mechanical, or other means, now known or hereafter invented, including
photocopying and recording, or in any information storage or retrieval system, without
permission in writing from the publishers.

Notice:
Product or corporate names may be trademarks or registered trademarks, and are used
only for identification and explanation without intent to infringe.

ISBN: 9781593633141 (pbk)

DOI: 10.4324/9781003236733

Contents

Contents

Teacher's Guide

Throughout history, mathematicians have been fascinated with puzzles and patterns. The *Rhind Papyrus* from Egypt is one of the oldest math texts ever found. It is basically a collection of puzzles. Puzzles are often made up of patterns that have led to many important mathematical discoveries. If you enjoyed the first *Math Puzzles and Patterns for Kids*, then get ready for more mathematical fun.

This book contains more of your favorite puzzles and patterns from the first book, as well as a few new ones for you to explore. All of the mathematical activities were chosen for their important roles in history and also because they can be simplified to a level for elementary students to understand. *More Math Puzzles and Patterns* focuses on practicing math skills within the context of discovering patterns and solving problems.

The lessons in this book may be used for a group study of math culture and history, or it can be used for independent skills practice to challenge an advanced student. The skills used in this book are based on the National Council of Teachers of Mathematics' (NCTM) *Principles for School Mathematics*. The Problem Solving standard will be addressed as students try to solve these puzzles and patterns. The patterns and relationships that students learn as they solve the puzzles and patterns will address NCTM's Algebra standard. Students will have the opportunity to practice their computational skills in addition, subtraction, and multiplication to address the Number and Operations standard, and they also will work with the Geometry Standard as they explore shape puzzles.

More Math Puzzles and Patterns is intended for students in grades 2–4, but the activities have also been used with some very advanced math students in first grade. First graders who want to take on the challenge might need a little help from a calculator. Students may work sequentially through the book, or teachers may select and reproduce certain sections to teach specific mathematical ideas. Other books related to mathematical puzzles are found in the Resources section at the back of the book. In addition, an Extension Activities section has been included to expand upon the puzzles and concepts in this book. Teachers also may use the answer key located at the end of the book to assess students' understanding of the math concepts.

I hope this book will encourage you to be a mathematician. Enjoy math and always look for the puzzles and patterns around you!

Name: _____ Date: _____

Fibonacci Sequence

The Fibonacci sequence is a famous set of numbers that form the following pattern: 1, 1, 2, 3, 5, 8, 13, 21. . . (and so on, infinitely). A sequence is a set of numbers that form a pattern.

1.) Can you figure out the pattern in Fibonacci's Sequence? How would you figure out the next number?

_____

_____

The Fibonacci sequence is sometimes called the "pinecone numbers." If you count the spirals on the bottom of a pinecone, you'll find that it always has a Fibonacci number of spirals. If you use a marker or paint to color each piece in the spiral, the spirals will be easier to see. The Fibonacci numbers appear in the spirals of sunflowers, artichokes, and pineapples, as well!

2.) Write the numbers that come next in Fibonacci's sequence.

1, 1, 2, 3, 5, 8, 13, 21, _____, _____, _____, _____, _____, _____, _____, _____

3.) Go on a nature hunt. Can you find other things in nature that come in sets of the Fibonacci sequence numbers?

1—   5—

2—   8—

3—poison ivy leaves   13—

© Taylor & Francis Group • *More Math Puzzles and Patterns for Kids*
This page may be photocopied or reproduced with permission for student use.

Name: _____ Date: _____

Fibonacci Sequence, Continued

These sequences follow the same pattern as the Fibonacci Sequence, but they begin with a different number. Fill in the missing numbers for each sequence.

1.)   2   ____   4   6   ____   16   26   ____

2.)   ____   ____   ____   15   25   40   ____   ____

3.)   ____   ____   6   9   ____   ____   39   63

4.)   ____   ____   ____   30   ____   80   130   ____

5.)   ____   8   ____   ____   ____   64   ____   ____

6.)   6   ____   ____   18   ____   48   78   ____

7.)   7   ____   ____   ____   35   ____   91   ____

8.)   4   4   ____   12   ____   32   52   ____

9.)   ____   ____   18   27   ____   72   ____   ____

10.)   15   15   ____   ____   ____   120   195   ____

11.)   11   11   22   ____   ____   ____   ____

12.)   25   25   ____   ____   ____   ____

13.)   100   100   ____   ____   ____   1,300   ____

14.)   ____   ____   42   ____   ____   ____   ____

15.)   12   ____   24   ____   ____   ____   ____

© Taylor & Francis Group • *More Math Puzzles and Patterns for Kids*
This page may be photocopied or reproduced with permission for student use.

Fibonacci Sequence, Continued

Complete the Fibonacci sequence backwards by subtracting.

1.) 21 13 _____ _____ _____ _____ _____ _____

Fill in the missing numbers of these similar subtraction sequences.

2.) 42 26 _____ _____ _____ _____ _____ _____

3.) 105 _____ 40 _____ _____ _____ _____ 5

4.) 189 117 _____ _____ 18 _____ _____

5.) 126 78 _____ _____ _____ 12 _____ 6

Use multiplication to complete these Fibonacci-style sequences.

6.) 2 2 _____ _____ _____

7.) 8 8 _____ _____ _____

8.) 5 5 _____ _____ _____

9.) 4 _____ _____ _____

10.) 12 _____ _____ _____ _____

Use division to solve the following sequences.

11.) 243 27 _____ _____ _____

12.) 59,049 729 _____ _____ _____

13.) 16,807 343 _____ _____ _____

14.) 7,776 216 _____ _____ _____

15.) 161,051 1,331 _____ _____ _____

© Taylor & Francis Group • *More Math Puzzles and Patterns for Kids*
This page may be photocopied or reproduced with permission for student use.

The Golden Rectangle

Fibonacci's sequence is also called the Golden Rectangle. The spiral formed in the rectangle will go on and on forever, a situation that mathematicians refer to as *infinity*. Infinity means never-ending.

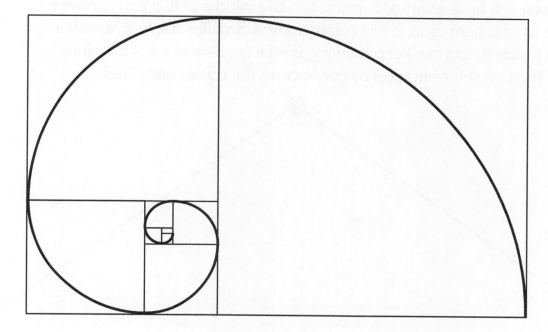

Some spiders use this spiral to form their webs. The sharp teeth and claws of some animals form the beginning of this spiral. Can you find other examples of spirals in nature? List your examples:

1.) _____

2.) _____

3.) _____

4.) _____

5.) _____

© Taylor & Francis Group • *More Math Puzzles and Patterns for Kids*
This page may be photocopied or reproduced with permission for student use.

Pentagon Star

In the same way that Fibonacci's Golden Rectangle will keep going forever and ever, a pentagon will also create an infinite number of stars. If you connect the points inside the pentagon with straight lines, you will draw a star. That star will have another pentagon in the middle of it. If you connect the points of that pentagon, it will create another smaller star with another pentagon inside it. You can keep drawing until it is so small you can't draw anymore. Try it on this pentagon by connecting the points with lines.

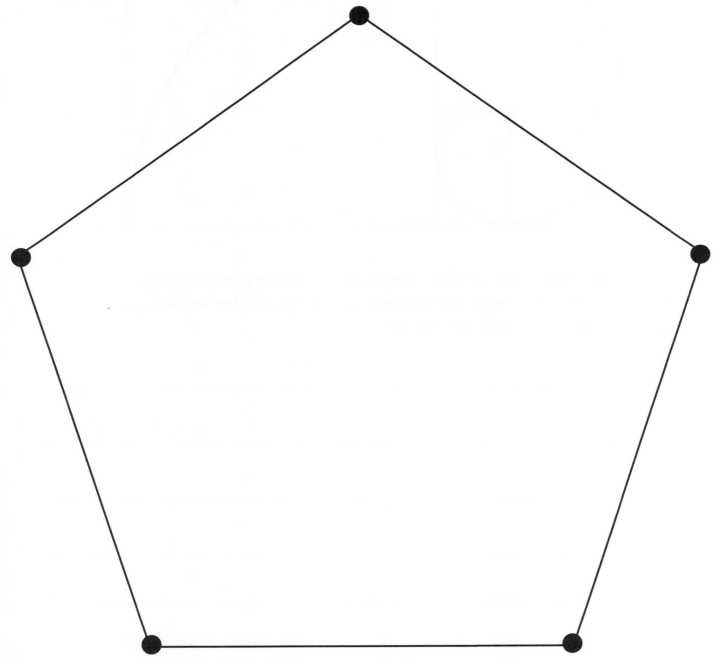

© Taylor & Francis Group • *More Math Puzzles and Patterns for Kids*
This page may be photocopied or reproduced with permission for student use.

The Binary Sequence

1.) The binary sequence is another famous set of numbers. Can you figure out the pattern?

1 , 2 , 4 , 8 , 16 , 32 , 64 , 128 , _____ , _____ , _____

2.) How did you figure out what comes next?

_____

_____

3.) Use the Venn diagram below to compare and contrast the numbers in the Binary Sequence to the numbers in the Fibonacci Sequence.

Binary sequence: 1, 2, 4, 8, 16, 32, 64, 128
Fibonacci sequence: 1, 1, 2, 3, 5, 8, 13, 21

Binary Sequence   Fibonacci Sequence

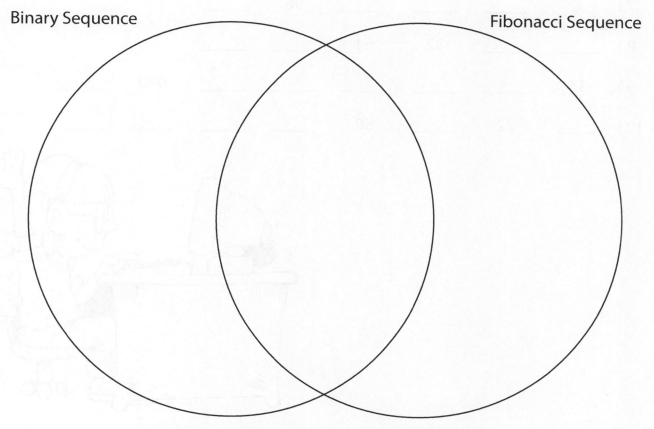

© Taylor & Francis Group • *More Math Puzzles and Patterns for Kids*
This page may be photocopied or reproduced with permission for student use.

The Binary Sequence, Continued

In the binary sequence, each number is doubled to get the next number. Write the number that comes next.

1.)   1   2   _____   _____   16   _____   _____   128

Try some similar doubling sequences that start with a different number.

2.)   3   6   12   _____   _____   96

3.)   9   _____   36   _____   _____   _____

4.)   5   _____   _____   40   _____   _____

5.)   4   8   16   _____   64   _____

6.)   _____   14   _____   56   112   _____

7.)   6   _____   _____   _____   96   _____

8.)   _____   _____   32   64   _____   _____

9.)   15   _____   _____   _____   _____   960   _____

10.)   _____   22   _____   88   _____   _____   _____

© Taylor & Francis Group • *More Math Puzzles and Patterns for Kids*
This page may be photocopied or reproduced with permission for student use.

The Binary Sequence, Continued

The numbers of the binary sequence are special because you can create any other number by adding together combinations of binary numbers. You can make every number from 1 to 127 using the first seven binary numbers:

1, 2, 4, 8, 16, 32, 64

For example, you can create 5 by adding 1 + 4. You can create 11 by adding 8 + 2 + 1.

Create the following numbers by adding combinations of binary numbers:

1.) 7 =

2.) 9 =

3.) 12 =

4.) 14 =

5.) 17 =

6.) 20 =

7.) 40 =

8.) 50 =

9.) 99 =

10.) 100 =

© Taylor & Francis Group • *More Math Puzzles and Patterns for Kids*
This page may be photocopied or reproduced with permission for student use.

Name: _____ Date: _____

The Binary Sequence, Continued

Create the Fibonacci numbers using combinations of the binary numbers:

1, 2, 4, 8, 16, 32, 64

1.) 1 =

2.) 2 =

3.) 3 =

4.) 5 =

5.) 8 =

6.) 13 =

7.) 21 =

8.) 34 =

9.) 55 =

10.) 89 =

© Taylor & Francis Group • *More Math Puzzles and Patterns for Kids*
This page may be photocopied or reproduced with permission for student use.

The Binary Sequence, Continued

Computers "think" by using the binary system. The binary numbers are used to form a binary system that uses only 0's and 1's to form numbers.

The number 1 is made up of one 1.
The number 2 is made up of zero 1's and one 2.
The number 3 is made up of one 1 and one 2.
The number 4 is made up of zero 1's, zero 2's and one 4.
The number 5 is made up of one 1, zero 2's and one 4.

Do you see the pattern? Each number can be made using either 0 or 1 of each binary number, beginning with 1 and increasing as needed. Complete the Binary System Chart of 0's and 1's for each number.

	1	2	4	8
1	1			
2	0	1		
3	1	1		
4	0	0	1	
5	1	0	1	
6				
7				
8				
9				
10				
11				
12				
13				
14				
15				

© Taylor & Francis Group • *More Math Puzzles and Patterns for Kids*
This page may be photocopied or reproduced with permission for student use.

Name: _____ Date: _____

Patterns in Multiplication

Finding patterns can help you solve math problems faster and easier. As you solve these problems, watch for a pattern.

1.) $0 \times 10 =$

2.) $1 \times 10 =$

3.) $2 \times 10 =$

4.) $3 \times 10 =$

5.) $4 \times 10 =$

6.) $5 \times 10 =$

7.) $6 \times 10 =$

8.) $7 \times 10 =$

9.) $8 \times 10 =$

10.) $9 \times 10 =$

Did you notice that when you multiply by 10, you just add a zero to the number by which you are multiplying? Use this pattern to solve the problems below.

11.) $13 \times 10 =$

12.) $42 \times 10 =$

13.) $579 \times 10 =$

14.) $1,789 \times 10 =$

15.) $6,011 \times 10 =$

16.) $9,000 \times 10 =$

17.) $10 \times 874 =$

18.) $10 \times 52 =$

19.) $10 \times 803 =$

20.) $10 \times 222 =$

© Taylor & Francis Group • *More Math Puzzles and Patterns for Kids*
This page may be photocopied or reproduced with permission for student use.

Patterns in Multiplication, Continued

1.) What do you think will happen when you multiply by 100?

_____

2.) $5 \times 100 =$

3.) $25 \times 100 =$

4.) $50 \times 100 =$

5.) $82 \times 100 =$

6.) $99 \times 100 =$

7.) $245 \times 100 =$

8.) $503 \times 100 =$

9.) $897 \times 100 =$

10.) $1,452 \times 100 =$

11.) $6,751 \times 100 =$

12.) What do you think will happen when you multiply by 1,000?

_____

13.) $8 \times 1,000 =$

14.) $46 \times 1,000 =$

15.) $9,523 \times 1,000 =$

16.) $893 \times 1,000 =$

17.) $89 \times 1,000 =$

18.) $194 \times 1,000 =$

19.) What will happen if you multiply by 100,000?

_____

20.) $953 \times 100,000 =$

21.) $2,659 \times 100,000 =$

22.) $7,002 \times 100,000 =$

23.) $370 \times 100,000 =$

24.) $1,000 \times 100,000 =$

25.) $83,420 \times 100,000 =$

© Taylor & Francis Group • *More Math Puzzles and Patterns for Kids*
This page may be photocopied or reproduced with permission for student use.

Patterns in Multiplication, Continued

Watch for a pattern when multiplying by 5.

1.) $2 \times 5 =$

2.) $4 \times 5 =$

3.) $6 \times 5 =$

4.) $8 \times 5 =$

5.) $10 \times 5 =$

6.) $40 \times 5 =$

Did you notice that when you multiply an even number by 5 the answer always has zero in the one's place? Did you notice that the digit in the ten's place is half of the number that you multiplied by 5?

Now multiply odd numbers by 5.

7.) $1 \times 5 =$

8.) $3 \times 5 =$

9.) $5 \times 5 =$

10.) $7 \times 5 =$

11.) $9 \times 5 =$

12.) $11 \times 5 =$

What digit is in the one's place when you multiply an odd number by 5? To get the ten's digit, subtract one from the number you are multiplying by five and divide it in half.

Use this trick to solve the following problems:

13.) $12 \times 5 =$

14.) $14 \times 5 =$

15.) $16 \times 5 =$

16.) $18 \times 5 =$

17.) $20 \times 5 =$

18.) $13 \times 5 =$

19.) $15 \times 5 =$

20.) $17 \times 5 =$

21.) $19 \times 5 =$

22.) $21 \times 5 =$

Pascal's Triangle

Pascal's triangle is a number pattern that is arranged in the form of a triangle. It starts with 1 at the top of the triangle. The other numbers are the sum of the 2 numbers above them.

1.) Complete the missing numbers in Pascal's triangle.

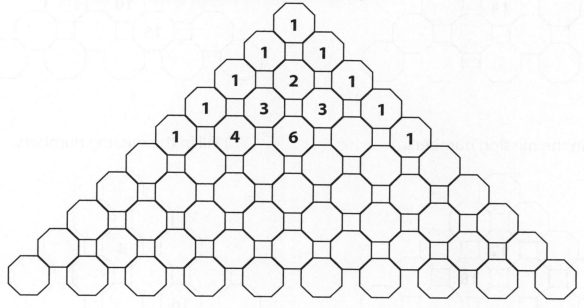

2.) Fill in the missing numbers for a triangle similar to Pascal's that starts with 10 at the top.

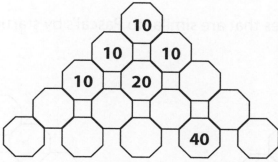

3.) Can you figure out what number this triangle begins with? Fill in the missing numbers.

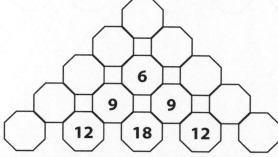

© Taylor & Francis Group • *More Math Puzzles and Patterns for Kids*
This page may be photocopied or reproduced with permission for student use.

Pascal's Triangle, Continued

4.) Fill in the missing numbers.

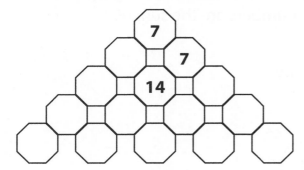

5.) Fill in the missing numbers.

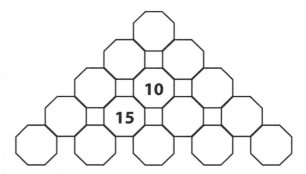

6.) Fill in the missing numbers.

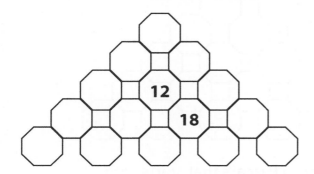

7.) Fill in the missing numbers.

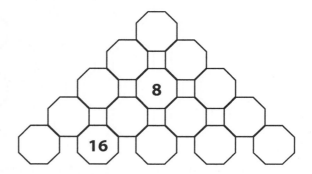

8.) Create your own triangles that are similar to Pascal's by starting with your favorite numbers.

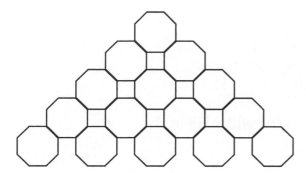

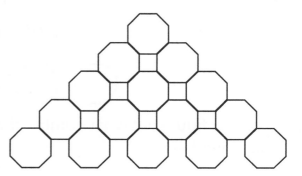

© Taylor & Francis Group • *More Math Puzzles and Patterns for Kids*
This page may be photocopied or reproduced with permission for student use.

Magic Triangles

Magic triangles have sides that add up to the same number. Triangles with three numbers on each side use each of the digits 1–6 once.

1.) If each side of this triangle has a sum of 9, can you figure out the missing numbers?

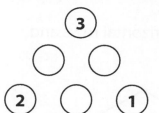

2.) Use the digits 1–6 to complete a magic triangle with sums of 12 on each side.

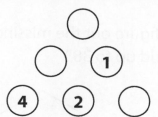

A magic triangle with four numbers on each side uses each of the digits 1–9 to create equal sums on each side.

3.) Fill in the missing numbers to complete this magic triangle with sums of 20 on each side.

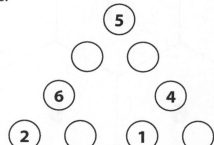

4.) Use each of the digits 1–9 to complete this magic triangle with sums of 23 on each side.

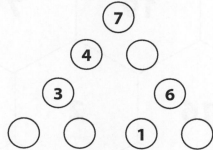

Use each of the digits 1–12 to complete these five-sided triangles.

5.) Complete this triangle with sums of 30 on each side.

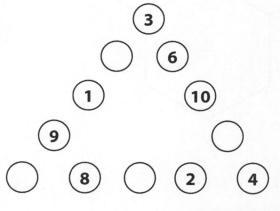

6.) Complete this triangle with sums of 28 on each side.

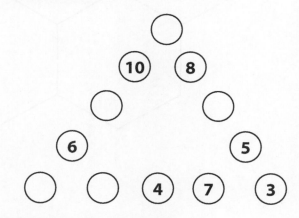

© Taylor & Francis Group • *More Math Puzzles and Patterns for Kids*
This page may be photocopied or reproduced with permission for student use.

Magic Hexagon

Many people have been fascinated by trying to create other "magic" shapes. The magic hexagon was first discovered by Ernst von Haselberg in 1887. All of the horizontal rows and diagonals within the shape add up to the same number.

1.) Can you figure out the missing numbers? (Hint: The horizontal rows and diagonals add up to 38.)

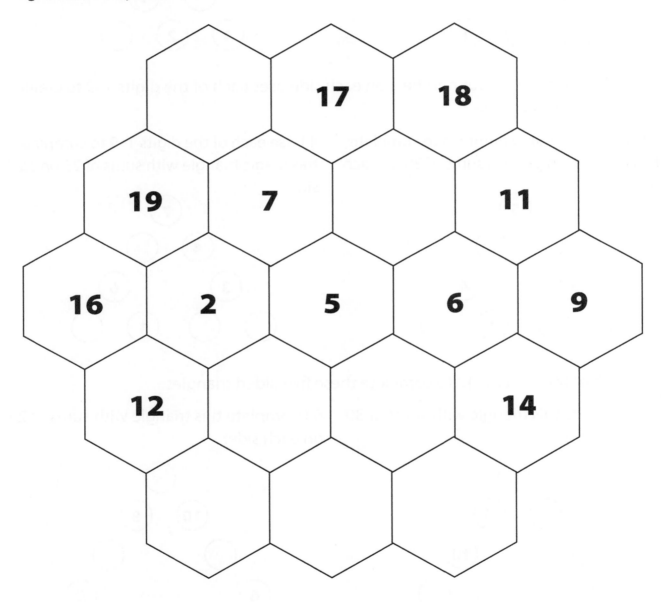

© Taylor & Francis Group • *More Math Puzzles and Patterns for Kids*
This page may be photocopied or reproduced with permission for student use.

Name: _____ Date: _____

Magic Squares

Magic squares have fascinated people for thousands of years. In a magic square, each row, column, and diagonal has the same sum. These squares use each of the digits 1–9 only once and have sums of 15.

Can you fill in the missing numbers?

1.)

2		6
		1
4	3	

2.)

	9	
	5	
8		6

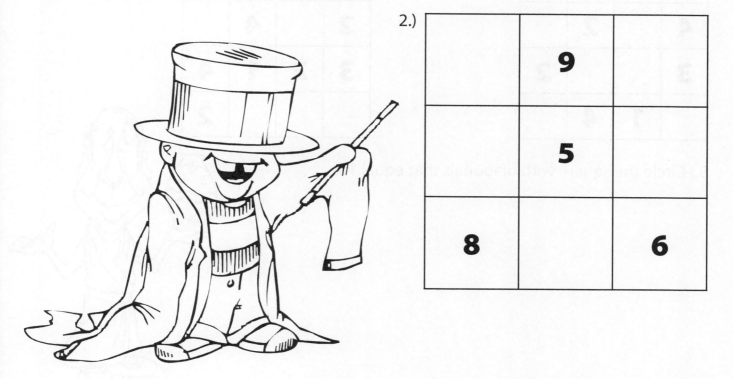

© Taylor & Francis Group • *More Math Puzzles and Patterns for Kids*
This page may be photocopied or reproduced with permission for student use.

Latin Squares

Latin squares are similar to magic squares, but only the columns and rows equal the same sum. Each number used in a Latin square must appear once in every row and column, but not more than once in the same row or column. These Latin squares use the numbers 1, 2, and 3 to create a sum of 6 in each row and column. Fill in the missing numbers.

1.)

1	2	3
	1	2

2.)

		3
1		2
	2	

These Latin squares also have sums of 10, but now they have four numbers on each side. Fill in the missing numbers.

3.)

	2	3	4
4		2	
3			2
	1	4	

4.)

4	1		3
2		4	
3	2	1	4
			2

5.) Circle the square with diagonals that equal 10.

© Taylor & Francis Group • *More Math Puzzles and Patterns for Kids*
This page may be photocopied or reproduced with permission for student use.

Latin Squares, Continued

Complete these Latin squares with 5 numbers on each side.

6.)

1	2	3		
2		5	1	
3		4	2	1
4			5	3
5	4	1		2

7.)

	5	1		2
5			1	3
4	1	3		
2		4	5	1
	2	5	3	

Now it's your turn! Create your own Latin squares in the grids below. Remember: Make sure the rows and columns add up to the same sum and that no number appears more than once in the same row or column.

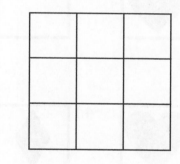

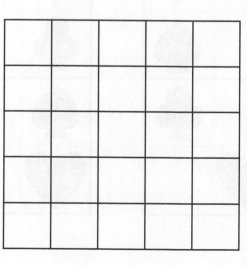

© Taylor & Francis Group • *More Math Puzzles and Patterns for Kids*
This page may be photocopied or reproduced with permission for student use.

Sudoku

A popular game in the form of a Latin square is called Sudoku. In Sudoku, each number must appear only once in every row and column. It also must appear only once in each 2 x 2 section of the square. These Sudoku puzzles use pictures instead of numbers. Draw pictures to complete the Sudoku puzzles.

1.)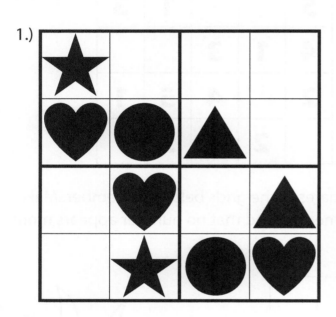

2.)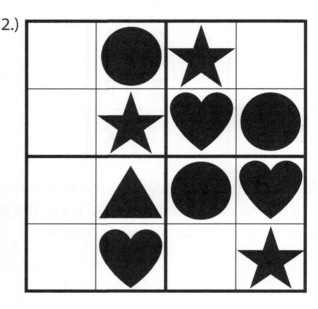

3.)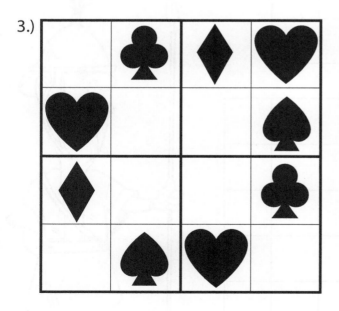

4.)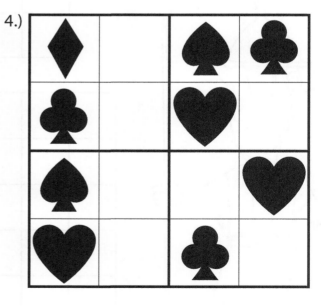

© Taylor & Francis Group • *More Math Puzzles and Patterns for Kids*
This page may be photocopied or reproduced with permission for student use.

Name: _____ Date: _____

Sudoku, Continued

These Sudoku puzzles use the numbers 1–4. Fill in the missing numbers.

5.)

	2	3	
3		2	1
	1		4
4	3	1	

6.)

		1	2
		3	4
4	3		
1	2		

Traditional Sudoku puzzles have 9 numbers in each row and column. Every 3 x 3 box must also have the numbers 1–9. Fill in the missing numbers of these Sudoku puzzles.

7.)

7	8	9	4	5	6	1	2	3
1	2		7	8	9		5	6
4	5	6	1		3	7	8	
	7	8	5	6	4	3	1	2
3	1	2	8	9	7		4	5
6	4		2	3		9	7	8
5	6	4	9		8	2	3	1
8	9		3	1	2	5		
	3	1	6	4	5		9	7

8.)

	6	9	5	8	2	1		4
2	5	8	4	7	1	3	9	
8		5	9	3	6		1	7
7	1	4		2	5	6	3	9
9	3	6	7	1	4	5	2	8
4	7	1	3	6	9	8	5	2
6		3	2	5	8	7	4	
	8	2	1	4	7	9	6	3

© Taylor & Francis Group • *More Math Puzzles and Patterns for Kids*
This page may be photocopied or reproduced with permission for student use.

Name: _____ Date: _____

Sudoku, Continued

Complete the Sudoku puzzles.

9.)

			7	8	9	4	5	6
6	5	4	1	2	3		8	
7	8			5		3	2	1
2	3	1	8	9	7	6	4	
5		6	2		1	7	9	8
	9	7	5	4	6		3	2
3	1		9		8	5		4
4	6		3	1	2		7	9
9	7	8	4	6	5	2	1	3

10.)

8			4	3	9	7		6
9	3	4	6	1	7		2	5
7	1	6		2	8	9	3	
1		7	8	5	2	3	4	9
	4	9		6	1	2	5	
	5	8	9		3		6	7
	7	1	2	8	5	4	9	
4		3	1	7	6	5	8	2
5	8	2	3		4	6		1

11.)

8	7	9		5	6	1		2
	6	4	3	2	1	7	9	8
2	1			8	7	6	4	5
1	3	2	8	7	9		5	6
6	4	5	2	1	3	9	8	
	9	8	5		4	3		
9		7		4	5	2	1	3
4	5	6		3	2		7	9
3		1	7		8		6	4

12.)

	2	8	4	9	3			6
4			6	7			8	5
6	1	7	5		2	3	9	4
7		1	8	2		4	3	9
8	5	2	9	3	4	6	1	7
9		3	7	1	6	5	2	
3	9	4	1	6		8	5	2
1	7		2	5	8		4	
	8	5	3		9	7	6	1

© Taylor & Francis Group • *More Math Puzzles and Patterns for Kids*
This page may be photocopied or reproduced with permission for student use.

Sudoku, Continued

Color the squares to complete the rainbow Sudoku. Every row, column, and 3 x 3 box should have one of each color.

13.)

Yellow	Red			Blue	Green	Purple	Pink	Brown
Black	Blue	Green	Purple	Pink			Red	Orange
Purple	Pink		Yellow	Red	Orange	Black	Blue	
Brown		Blue	Green	Yellow		Orange		Pink
Green	Yellow	Red	Orange	Purple	Pink	Brown	Black	Blue
	Purple	Pink		Black	Blue	Green	Yellow	
Blue	Green	Yellow	Pink	Brown	Black		Orange	Purple
	Brown	Black	Red		Purple	Blue	Green	
Red	Orange			Green		Pink	Brown	Black

Sudoku, Continued

Color the squares to complete another rainbow Sudoku.

14.)

Purple	Yellow		Orange	Green		Red		Pink
Red	Blue	Pink	Yellow	Black	Purple	Green	Brown	Orange
	Green	Brown		Blue	Pink	Yellow	Black	
Black		Yellow	Brown	Orange			Red	Blue
Brown	Orange	Green	Pink	Red	Blue	Purple	Yellow	Black
Pink		Blue	Purple		Black	Orange		Brown
	Black	Purple	Green		Orange		Pink	Red
Green	Brown		Blue	Pink	Red	Black	Purple	Yellow
Blue	Pink	Red		Purple	Yellow	Brown	Orange	

© Taylor & Francis Group • *More Math Puzzles and Patterns for Kids*
This page may be photocopied or reproduced with permission for student use.

The Eight Queens Puzzle

The Eight Queens puzzle was developed by a chess player and has been worked by many mathematicians. Place eight queens on the chess board so that no queen is in the same row, column, or diagonal as another queen. Can you figure out where the missing queen belongs on each of these Eight Queens puzzles? Draw the missing queen or write a letter Q.

1.)

© Taylor & Francis Group • *More Math Puzzles and Patterns for Kids*
This page may be photocopied or reproduced with permission for student use.

Name: _____   Date: _____

The Eight Queens Puzzle, Continued

This Eight Queens puzzle is missing two queens. Remember that no queen can be in the same row, column, or diagonal as another queen. Draw the two missing queens on each chess board.

2.)

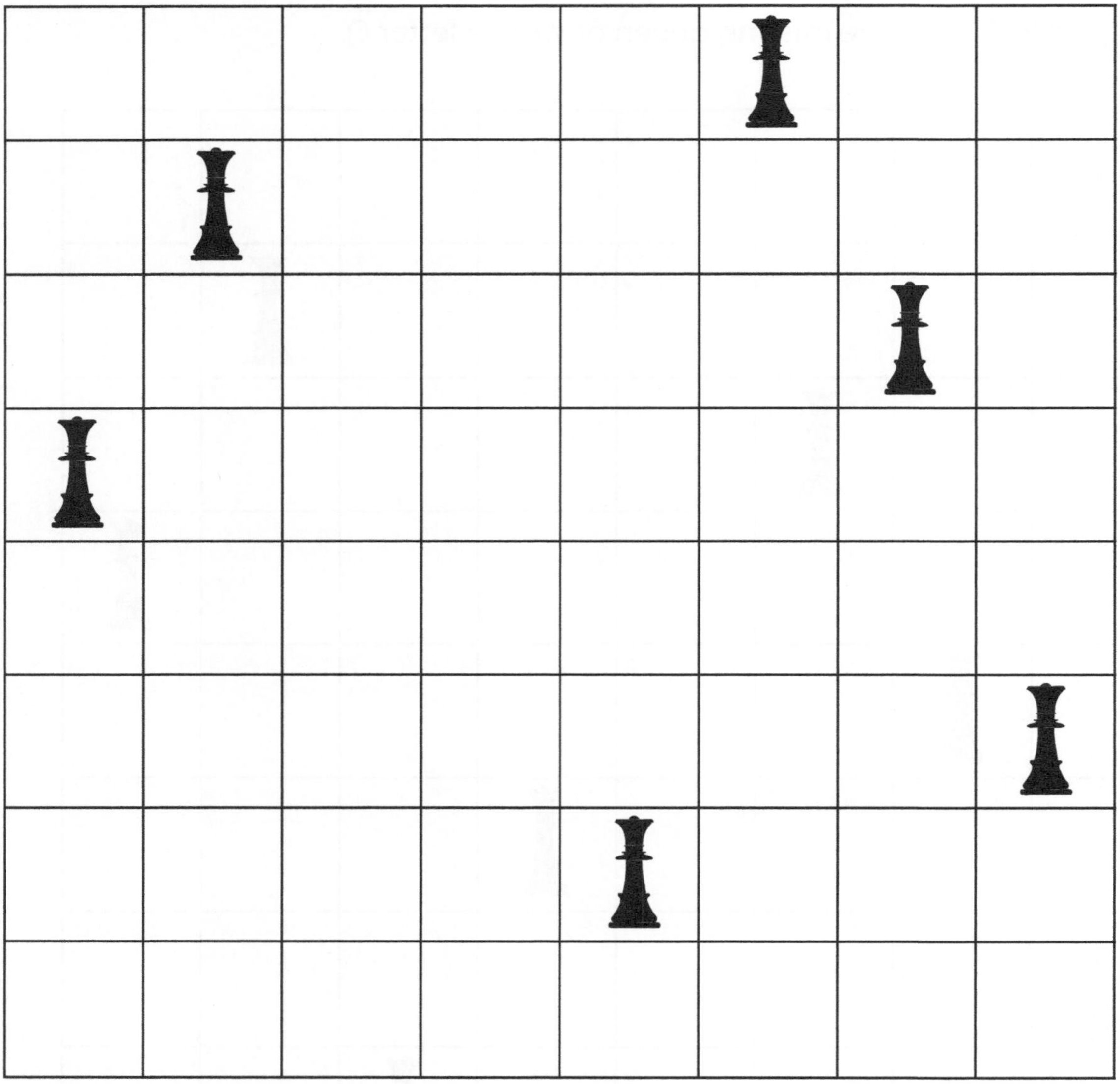

Name: _____ Date: _____

The Eight Queens Puzzle, Continued

This Eight Queens puzzle is missing two queens. Remember that no queen can be in the same row, column, or diagonal as another queen. Draw the two missing queens on each chess board.

3.)

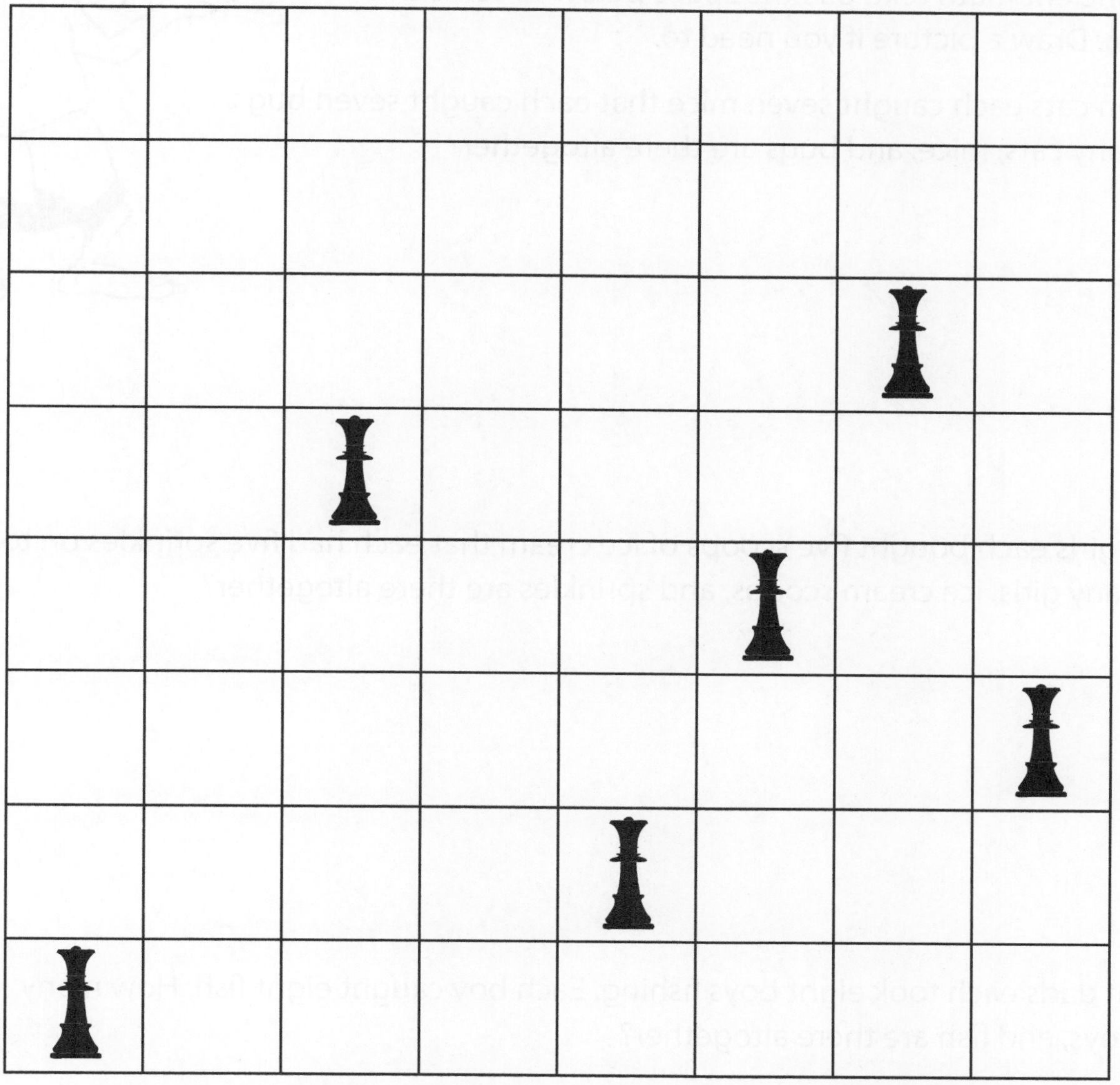

Name: _____ Date: _____

The Rhind Papyrus

The *Rhind Papyrus* found in Egypt had puzzle-type word problems. Papyrus was a material the Egyptians used to write on, much like we use paper today. The following problem is similar to a problem found in this ancient math text. Use the space below to solve this problem. Draw a picture if you need to.

1.) Seven cats each caught seven mice that each caught seven bugs. How many cats, mice, and bugs are there altogether?

2.) Five girls each bought five scoops of ice cream that each had five sprinkles on top. How many girls, ice cream scoops, and sprinkles are there altogether?

3.) Eight dads each took eight boys fishing. Each boy caught eight fish. How many dads, boys, and fish are there altogether?

© Taylor & Francis Group • *More Math Puzzles and Patterns for Kids*
This page may be photocopied or reproduced with permission for student use.

The Rhind Papyrus, Continued

4.) Four kings each had four sons who each had four dogs that each had four bones. How many kings, sons, dogs, and bones are there altogether?

5.) Three queens each had three daughters who each had three dolls that each had three gowns. How many queens, daughters, dolls, and gowns are there altogether?

6.) Six children were each given six sacks that each contained six oranges that each had six seeds. How many children, sacks, oranges, and seeds are there altogether?

© Taylor & Francis Group • *More Math Puzzles and Patterns for Kids*
This page may be photocopied or reproduced with permission for student use.

Name: _____ Date: _____

Kirkman's School Girl Problem

Kirkman's School Girl problem is another famous word problem. He asked how a certain number of girls could walk to school a certain number of days, but walk with a different group of girls each day. Try a problem that is similar to this famous problem.

1.) Maria, Jennifer, Dora, Ling, Amber, Kayla, Nicole, and Tiffany are eight girls that walk to school each day. Show how the girls can walk with a different partner each day for a week.

Monday	
Maria	Jennifer
Dora	Ling
Amber	Kayla
Nicole	Tiffany

Tuesday	

Wednesday	

Thursday	

Friday	

© Taylor & Francis Group • *More Math Puzzles and Patterns for Kids*
This page may be photocopied or reproduced with permission for student use.

Name: _____ Date: _____

Kirkman's School Girl Problem, Continued

2.) Eight boys meet after school each day to play chess. They like to play with a different partner each day. Can you arrange the boys in different groups of two for each day of the week?

Monday	
Matthew	Brandon
Tony	Carlos
Lee	David
Shane	Henry

Tuesday	

Wednesday	

Thursday	

Friday	

Tangrams

Tangrams are ancient puzzles from China. A square is cut into seven pieces, two large triangles, one medium triangle, two small triangles, one square, and one parallelogram. One challenge of a tangram is to put the seven pieces back together into the square. The seven pieces also can be rearranged without overlapping to make other shapes. People often make up stories as they create shapes. Cut out the seven shape pieces and rearrange them to make pictures.

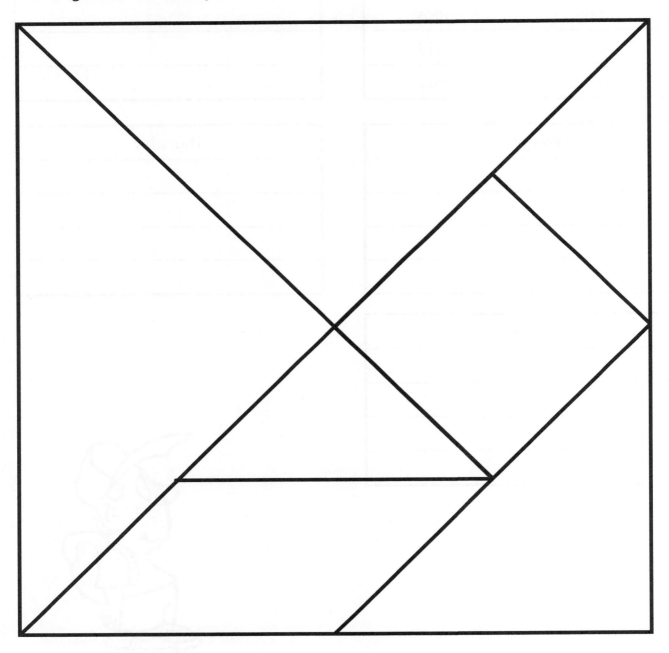

© Taylor & Francis Group • *More Math Puzzles and Patterns for Kids*
This page may be photocopied or reproduced with permission for student use.

Tangrams, Continued

List five different pictures you can make with the Tangram pieces, and make a small sketch of each arrangement.

1.)

2.)

3.)

4.)

5.)

© Taylor & Francis Group • *More Math Puzzles and Patterns for Kids*
This page may be photocopied or reproduced with permission for student use.

The Loculus of Archimedes

The loculus of Archimedes is one of the oldest puzzles ever found. It also is called Stomachion. Archimedes, who created the loculus, was one of the first mathematicians to simplify math by creating models of the problems. As with the tangrams, cut out the pieces and rearrange them to create new pictures using all 14 pieces. An elephant is a popular picture to make with the loculus pieces.

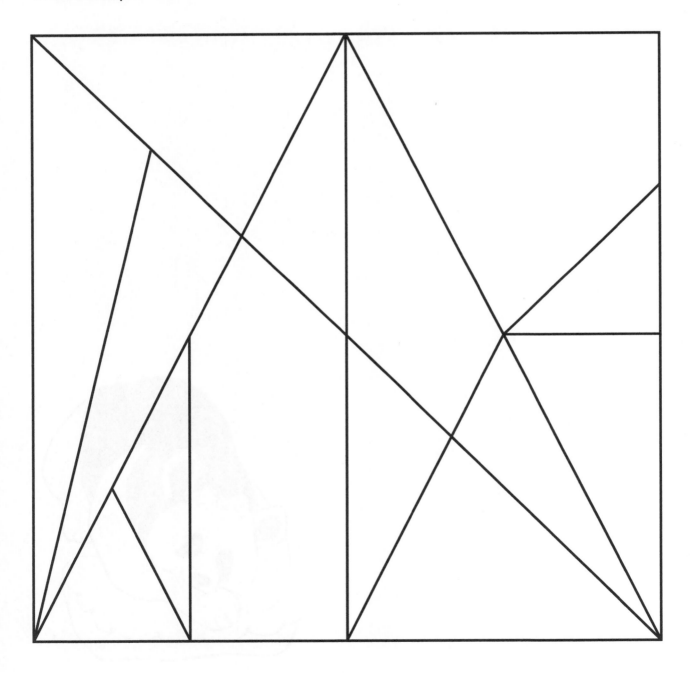

© Taylor & Francis Group • *More Math Puzzles and Patterns for Kids*
This page may be photocopied or reproduced with permission for student use.

The Loculus of Archimedes, Continued

List five different pictures you can make with the loculus pieces, and make a small sketch of each arrangement:

1.)

2.)

3.)

4.)

5.)

What Have You Learned About Math?

Hopefully as you completed this workbook, you learned a few interesting facts about the history of math and famous mathematicians. You should have learned some math terms and recognized that puzzles and patterns have a mathematical connection. Use the words in the box to complete the sentences below.

magic hexagon	binary sequence	Archimedes	Kirkman	Pascal
Eight Queens	pentagon	*Rhind Papyrus*	Infinity	Fibonacci sequence

1.) The _____ puzzle is based on the board game chess.

2.) Computers use the _____ .

3.) The _____ is one of the oldest math texts discovered.

4.) _____ means to go on forever and ever.

5.) A _____ has five corners that form a star when connected.

6.) _____ is a famous mathematician who created a puzzle like tangrams.

7.) _____ developed a math problem about school girls.

8.) Ernst von Haselberg discovered the

_____.

9.) _____ created a number pattern in the form of a triangle.

10.) The "pinecone numbers" are found in the

_____.

© Taylor & Francis Group • *More Math Puzzles and Patterns for Kids*
This page may be photocopied or reproduced with permission for student use.

Resources

Archimedes' Square, "Stomachion": The world's oldest known puzzle" (n.d.). Retrieved September 2, 2007, from http://www.gamepuzzles.com/archsqu.htm

Castor, H. (1995). *Starting chess*. New York: Scholastic.

Danesi, M. (2002). *The puzzle instinct: The meaning of puzzles in human life*. Bloomington, IN: University Press.

Hulme, J. N. (2005). *Wild Fibonacci: Nature's secret code revealed*. Berkeley, CA: Tricycle Press.

Knott, R. (2007). *Fibonacci numbers and the golden section*. Retrieved September 9, 2007, from http://www.mcs.surrey.ac.uk/Personal/R.Knott/Fibonacci/fib.html

Murphy, F. (2001). *Ben Franklin and the magic squares*. New York: Random House.

Schwartz, D. M. (1998). *G is for googol: A math alphabet book*. Berkeley, CA: Tricycle Press.

Smith, S. (1996). *Agnesi to zeno: Over 100 vignettes from the history of math*. Emeryville, CA: Key Curriculum Press.

Stomachion. (n.d.). Retrieved September 2, 2007, from http://www.geocities.com/tangramfan/stomachion.html

Tompart, A. (1990). *Grandfather Tang's story*. New York: Crown.

Weisstein, E. W. (2003). *Stomachion*. Retrieved September 2, 2007, from http://mathworld.wolfram.com/Stomachion.html

Wright, A. (1997) *Alice in pastaland: A math adventure*. Watertown, MA: Charlesbridge.

Extension Activities

1.) Archimedes was a famous Greek mathematician. Research to discover some of his important contributions and inventions. He made the expression "Eureka!" famous. Find out why.

2.) Mathematicians often make models or drawings to solve problems. Use models and drawings to help you solve puzzles in this book:
  - Use masking tape to make a grid on the floor for solving the various square problems (magic squares, Sudoku, and Eight Queens). Write the numbers (or pictures) on index cards that you can move around to help you solve the puzzle.
  - Use a real chess board and eight game pieces to help solve the Eight Queens problem. In the game of chess, queens can attack horizontally, vertically, and diagonally.
  - Use poster paper to prove your answers to the *Rhind Papyrus* problems by drawing pictures to show the solution.
  - Use puppets, dolls, or friends to act out the Kirkman School Girl problems.

3.) Create your own problems and challenge friends to solve them:
  - Create your own tangram or loculus-style puzzle. Start with a square and cut it into various shapes.
  - Create your own number patterns and have your friends solve them.
  - Create your own story problems and have your friends solve them.
  - Use a chess board and eight game pieces to create your own solution to the Eight Queens problem.

4.) Learn how to play chess. Research the moves of the other game pieces.
  - After you find out how the other game pieces attack, try making your own game similar to the Eight Queens puzzle. How many knights can you put on a chess board so that none can attack another?
  - Can you figure out how many squares are on a chess board? At first, you might count 64, but remember, the whole board makes one big square, four small squares make a square, 16 small squares make a bigger square, and so on. Make several copies of a chess board and color all of the squares you find using different colors.

Answer Key

Fibonacci Sequence, p. 6

1.) Each number is the sum of the two previous numbers.
2.) 1, 1, 2, 3, 5, 8, 13, 21, 34, 55, 89, 144, 233, 377, 610, 987
3.) Answers will vary. Some examples are: starfish (5 arms), octopus (8 tentacles), spiders (8 legs), your body (2 eyes, 2 ears, 1 nose, 5 fingers on each hand—or 8 fingers and 2 thumbs total), apple (5 sections), and most flowers have a Fibonacci number of petals.

Fibonacci Sequence, Continued, p. 7

1.) 2; 2; 4; 6; 10; 16; 26; 42
2.) 5; 5; 10; 15; 25; 40; 65; 105
3.) 3; 3; 6; 9; 15; 24; 39; 63
4.) 10; 10; 20; 30; 50; 80; 130; 210
5.) 8; 8; 16; 24; 40; 64; 104; 168
6.) 6; 6; 12; 18; 30; 48; 78; 126
7.) 7; 7; 14; 21; 35; 56; 91; 147
8.) 4; 4; 8; 12; 20; 32; 52; 84
9.) 9; 9; 18; 27; 45; 72; 117; 189
10.) 15; 15; 30; 45; 75; 120; 195; 315
11.) 11; 11; 22; 33; 55; 88; 143; 231
12.) 25; 25; 50; 75; 125; 200; 325; 525
13.) 100; 100; 200; 300; 500; 800; 1,300; 2,100
14.) 21; 21; 42; 63; 105; 168; 273; 441
15.) 12; 12; 24; 36; 60; 96; 156; 252

Fibonacci Sequence, Continued, p. 8

1.) 21; 13; 8; 5; 3; 2; 1; 1
2.) 42; 26; 16; 10; 6; 4; 2; 2
3.) 105; 65; 40; 25; 15; 10; 5; 5
4.) 189; 117; 72; 45; 27; 18; 9; 9
5.) 126; 78; 48; 30; 18; 12; 6; 6
6.) 2; 2; 4; 8; 32
7.) 8; 8; 64; 512; 32,768
8.) 5; 5; 25; 125; 3,125
9.) 4; 4; 16; 64; 1,024
10.) 12; 12; 144; 1,728; 248,832
11.) 243; 27; 9; 3; 3
12.) 59,049; 729; 81; 9; 9
13.) 16,807; 343; 49; 7; 7
14.) 7,776; 216; 36; 6; 6
15.) 161,051; 1,331; 121; 11; 11

The Golden Rectangle, p. 9

1–5.) Answers will vary. Some examples include: shells of snails and of marine mollusks; spiraled horns of a mountain goat; the arrangement of seeds in the heads of sunflowers and daisies; and galaxies.

Pentagon Star, p. 10

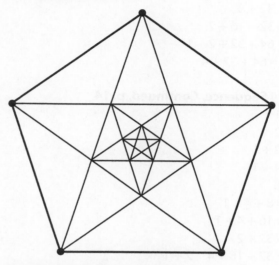

The Binary Sequence, p. 11

1.) 1; 2; 4; 8; 16; 32; 64; 128; 256; 512; 1,024
2.) Each number is the sum of the previous number doubled.
3.)

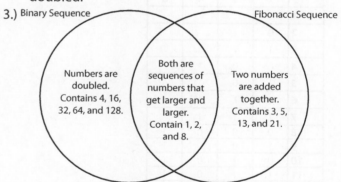

Binary Sequence — Numbers are doubled. Contains 4, 16, 32, 64, and 128.
Both are sequences of numbers that get larger and larger. Contain 1, 2, and 8.
Fibonacci Sequence — Two numbers are added together. Contains 3, 5, 13, and 21.

The Binary Sequence, Continued, p. 12

1.) 1; 2; 4; 8; 16; 32; 64; 128
2.) 3; 6; 12; 24; 48; 96
3.) 9; 18; 36; 72; 144; 288
4.) 5; 10; 20; 40; 80; 160
5.) 4; 8; 16; 32; 64; 128
6.) 7; 14; 28; 56; 112; 224
7.) 6; 12; 24; 48; 96; 192
8.) 8; 16; 32; 64; 128; 256
9.) 15; 30; 60; 120; 240; 480; 960; 1,920
10.) 11; 22; 44; 88; 176; 352; 704; 1,408

The Binary Sequence, Continued, p. 13

1.) $7 = 4 + 2 + 1$
2.) $9 = 8 + 1$
3.) $12 = 8 + 4$
4.) $14 = 8 + 2 + 4$
5.) $17 = 16 + 1$
6.) $20 = 16 + 4$
7.) $40 = 32 + 8$
8.) $50 = 32 + 16 + 2$
9.) $99 = 64 + 32 + 2 + 1$
10.) $100 = 64 + 32 + 4$

The Binary Sequence, Continued, p. 14

1.) $1 = 1$
2.) $2 = 2$
3.) $3 = 2 + 1$
4.) $5 = 4 + 1$
5.) $8 = 8$
6.) $13 = 8 + 4 + 1$
7.) $21 = 16 + 4 + 1$
8.) $34 = 32 + 2$
9.) $55 = 32 + 16 + 4 + 2 + 1$
10.) $89 = 64 + 16 + 8 + 1$

The Binary Sequence, Continued, p. 15

	1	2	4	8
1	1			
2	0	1		
3	1	1		
4	0	0	1	
5	1	0	1	
6	0	1	1	
7	1	1	1	
8	0	0	0	1
9	1	0	0	1
10	0	1	0	1
11	1	1	0	1
12	0	0	1	1
13	1	0	1	1
14	0	1	1	1
15	1	1	1	1

Patterns in Multiplication, p. 16

1.) $0 \times 10 = 0$
2.) $1 \times 10 = 10$
3.) $2 \times 10 = 20$
4.) $3 \times 10 = 30$
5.) $4 \times 10 = 40$
6.) $5 \times 10 = 50$
7.) $6 \times 10 = 60$
8.) $7 \times 10 = 70$
9.) $8 \times 10 = 80$
10.) $9 \times 10 = 90$
11.) $13 \times 10 = 130$
12.) $42 \times 10 = 420$
13.) $579 \times 10 = 5,790$
14.) $1,789 \times 10 = 17,890$
15.) $6,011 \times 10 = 60,110$
16.) $9,000 \times 10 = 90,000$
17.) $10 \times 874 = 8,740$
18.) $10 \times 52 = 520$
19.) $10 \times 803 = 8,030$
20.) $10 \times 222 = 2,220$

Patterns in Multiplication, Continued, p. 17

1.) Add 2 zeros to the number by which you are multiplying.
2.) $5 \times 100 = 500$
3.) $25 \times 100 = 2,500$
4.) $50 \times 100 = 5,000$
5.) $82 \times 100 = 8,200$
6.) $99 \times 100 = 9,900$
7.) $245 \times 100 = 24,500$
8.) $503 \times 100 = 50,300$
9.) $897 \times 100 = 89,700$
10.) $1,452 \times 100 = 145,200$
11.) $6,751 \times 100 = 675,100$
12.) Add 3 zeros to the number by which you are multiplying.
13.) $8 \times 1,000 = 8,000$
14.) $46 \times 1,000 = 46,000$
15.) $9,523 \times 1,000 = 9,523,000$
16.) $893 \times 1,000 = 893,000$
17.) $89 \times 1,000 = 89,000$
18.) $194 \times 1,000 = 194,000$
19.) Add 5 zeros to the number by which you are multiplying.
20.) $953 \times 100,000 = 95,300,000$
21.) $2,659 \times 100,000 = 265,900,000$
22.) $7,002 \times 100,000 = 700,200,000$
23.) $370 \times 100,000 = 37,000,000$
24.) $1,000 \times 100,000 = 100,000,000$
25.) $83,420 \times 100,000 = 8,342,000,000$

Patterns in Multiplication, Continued, p. 18

1.) $2 \times 5 = 10$
2.) $4 \times 5 = 20$
3.) $6 \times 5 = 30$
4.) $8 \times 5 = 40$
5.) $10 \times 5 = 50$
6.) $40 \times 5 = 200$
7.) $1 \times 5 = 5$
8.) $3 \times 5 = 15$
9.) $5 \times 5 = 25$
10.) $7 \times 5 = 35$
11.) $9 \times 5 = 45$
12.) $11 \times 5 = 55$
13.) $12 \times 5 = 60$
14.) $14 \times 5 = 70$
15.) $16 \times 5 = 80$
16.) $18 \times 5 = 90$
17.) $20 \times 5 = 100$
18.) $13 \times 5 = 65$
19.) $15 \times 5 = 75$
20.) $17 \times 5 = 85$
21.) $19 \times 5 = 95$
22.) $21 \times 5 = 105$

Pascal's Triangle, pp. 19–20

1.)

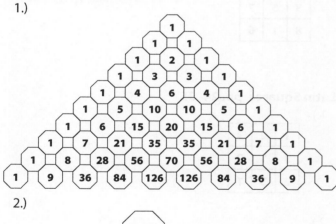

2.)

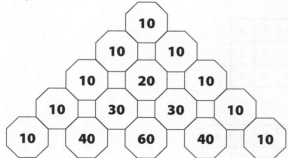

3.)

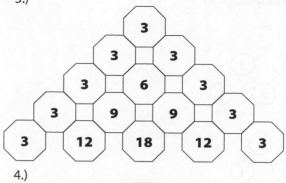

4.)

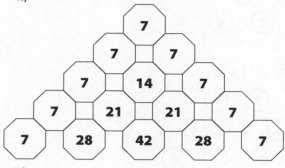

5.)

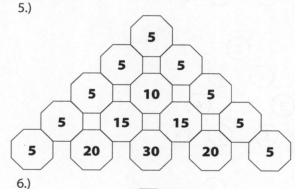

6.)

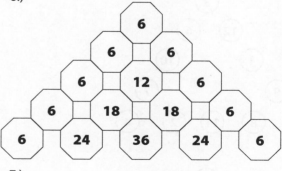

7.)

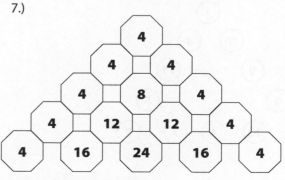

8.)   Answers will vary.

Magic Triangles, p. 21

1.)
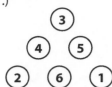

2.)
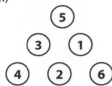

3.)
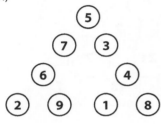

4.)
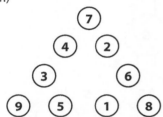

5.)
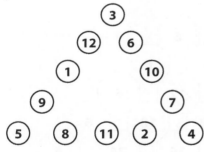

6.)
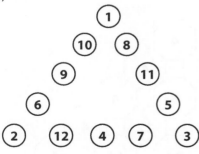

Magic Hexagon, p. 22

1.)
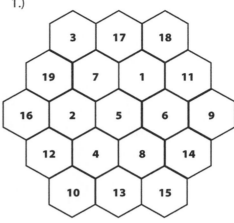

Magic Squares, p. 23

1.)

2	7	6
9	5	1
4	3	8

2.)

4	9	2
3	5	7
8	1	6

Latin Squares, pp. 24–25

1.)

1	2	3
3	1	2
2	3	1

2.)

2	1	3
1	3	2
3	2	1

3.)

1	2	3	4
4	3	2	1
3	4	1	2
2	1	4	3

4.)

4	1	2	3
2	3	4	1
3	2	1	4
1	4	3	2

5.) Square number 4 should be circled.

6.)

1	2	3	4	5
2	3	5	1	4
3	5	4	2	1
4	1	2	5	3
5	4	1	3	2

7.)

3	5	1	4	2
5	4	2	1	3
4	1	3	2	5
2	3	4	5	1
1	2	5	3	4

Sudoku, pp. 26–30

1.)

2.)

3.)

4.)

5.)

1	2	4	3
3	4	2	1
2	1	3	4
4	3	1	2

6.)

3	4	1	2
2	1	3	4
4	3	2	1
1	2	4	3

7.)

7	8	9	4	5	6	1	2	3
1	2	3	7	8	9	4	5	6
4	5	6	1	2	3	7	8	9
9	7	8	5	6	4	3	1	2
3	1	2	8	9	7	6	4	5
6	4	5	2	3	1	9	7	8
5	6	4	9	7	8	2	3	1
8	9	7	3	1	2	5	6	4
2	3	1	6	4	5	8	9	7

Sudoku, pp. 26–30, Continued

8.)

1	4	7	6	9	3	2	8	5
3	6	9	5	8	2	1	7	4
2	5	8	4	7	1	3	9	6
8	2	5	9	3	6	4	1	7
7	1	4	8	2	5	6	3	9
9	3	6	7	1	4	5	2	8
4	7	1	3	6	9	8	5	2
6	9	3	2	5	8	7	4	1
5	8	2	1	4	7	9	6	3

9.)

1	2	3	7	8	9	4	5	6
6	5	4	1	2	3	9	8	7
7	8	9	6	5	4	3	2	1
2	3	1	8	9	7	6	4	5
5	4	6	2	3	1	7	9	8
8	9	7	5	4	6	1	3	2
3	1	2	9	7	8	5	6	4
4	6	5	3	1	2	8	7	9
9	7	8	4	6	5	2	1	3

10.)

8	2	5	4	3	9	7	1	6
9	3	4	6	1	7	8	2	5
7	1	6	5	2	8	9	3	4
1	6	7	8	5	2	3	4	9
3	4	9	7	6	1	2	5	8
2	5	8	9	4	3	1	6	7
6	7	1	2	8	5	4	9	3
4	9	3	1	7	6	5	8	2
5	8	2	3	9	4	6	7	1

11.)

8	7	9	4	5	6	1	3	2
5	6	4	3	2	1	7	9	8
2	1	3	9	8	7	6	4	5
1	3	2	8	7	9	4	5	6
6	4	5	2	1	3	9	8	7
7	9	8	5	6	4	3	2	1
9	8	7	6	4	5	2	1	3
4	5	6	1	3	2	8	7	9
3	2	1	7	9	8	5	6	4

12.)

5	2	8	4	9	3	1	7	6
4	3	9	6	7	1	2	8	5
6	1	7	5	8	2	3	9	4
7	6	1	8	2	5	4	3	9
8	5	2	9	3	4	6	1	7
9	4	3	7	1	6	5	2	8
3	9	4	1	6	7	8	5	2
1	7	6	2	5	8	9	4	3
2	8	5	3	4	9	7	6	1

13.)

Yellow	Red	Orange	Black	Blue	Green	Purple	Pink	Brown
Black	Blue	Green	Purple	Pink	Brown	Yellow	Red	Orange
Purple	Pink	Brown	Yellow	Red	Orange	Black	Blue	Green
Brown	Black	Blue	Green	Yellow	Red	Orange	Purple	Pink
Green	Yellow	Red	Orange	Purple	Pink	Brown	Black	Blue
Orange	Purple	Pink	Brown	Black	Blue	Green	Yellow	Red
Blue	Green	Yellow	Pink	Brown	Black	Red	Orange	Purple
Pink	Brown	Black	Red	Orange	Purple	Blue	Green	Yellow
Red	Orange	Purple	Blue	Green	Yellow	Pink	Brown	Black

14.)

Purple	Yellow	Black	Orange	Green	Brown	Red	Blue	Pink
Red	Blue	Pink	Yellow	Black	Purple	Green	Brown	Orange
Orange	Green	Brown	Red	Blue	Pink	Yellow	Black	Purple
Black	Purple	Yellow	Brown	Orange	Green	Pink	Red	Blue
Brown	Orange	Green	Pink	Red	Blue	Purple	Yellow	Black
Pink	Red	Blue	Purple	Yellow	Black	Orange	Green	Brown
Yellow	Black	Purple	Green	Brown	Orange	Blue	Pink	Red
Green	Brown	Orange	Blue	Pink	Red	Black	Purple	Yellow
Blue	Pink	Red	Black	Purple	Yellow	Brown	Orange	Green

3.)

The Eight Queens Puzzle, pp. 31–33

1.)

2.)

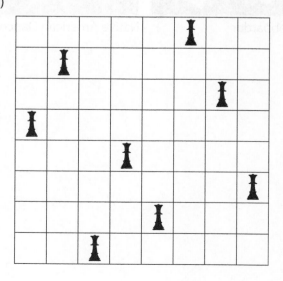

The Rhind Papyrus, p. 34–35

1.) 399 total
2.) 155 total
3.) 584 total
4.) 340 total
5.) 120 total
6.) 1,554 total

Kirkman's School Girl Problem, pp. 36–37

Answers may vary. Here are some possible solutions:

1.) Monday: Maria–Jennifer; Dora–Ling; Amber–Kayla; Nicole–Tiffany

Tuesday: Maria–Ling; Dora–Kayla; Amber–Tiffany; Nicole–Jennifer

Wednesday: Maria–Nicole; Amber–Dora; Kayla–Ling; Jennifer–Tiffany

Thursday: Maria–Kayla; Dora–Tiffany; Amber–Jennifer; Nicole–Ling

Friday: Maria–Dora; Amber–Nicole; Kayla–Tiffany; Jennifer–Ling

2.) Monday: Matthew–Brandon; Tony–Carlos; Lee–David; Shane–Henry

Tuesday: Matthew–David; Tony–Henry; Lee–Brandon; Shane–Carlos

Wednesday: Matthew–Tony; Lee–Shane; Henry–Brandon; David–Carlos

Thursday: Matthew–Carlos; Tony–David; Lee–Henry; Shane–Brandon

Friday: Matthew–Henry; Tony–Brandon; Lee–Carlos; Shane–David

Tangrams, pp. 38–39

Answers 1–5 will vary. See examples below.

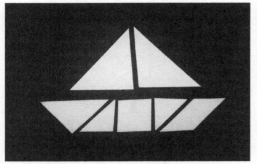

Sailboat

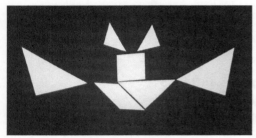

Bat

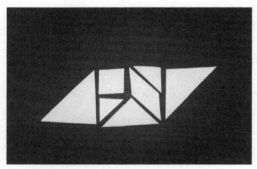

Parallelogram

Bird

The Loculus of Archimedes, pp. 40–41

Answers 1–5 will vary. See examples below.

Space Shuttle

Elephant

Skateboarder

Native American Dancer

MORE MATH PUZZLES AND PATTERNS FOR KIDS

What Have You Learned About Math?, p. 42

1.) The **Eight Queens** puzzle is based on the board game Chess.
2.) Computers use the **binary sequence**.
3.) The ***Rhind Papyrus*** is one of the oldest math texts discovered.
4.) **Infinity** means to go on forever and ever.
5.) A **pentagon** has five corners that form a star when connected.
6.) **Archimedes** is a famous mathematician who created a puzzle like tangrams.
7.) **Kirkman** developed a math problem about school girls.
8.) Ernst von Haselberg discovered the **magic hexagon**.
9.) **Pascal** created a number pattern in the form of a triangle.
10.) The "pinecone numbers" are found in the **Fibonacci sequence**.

About the Author

Kristy Fulton, author of *Math Puzzles and Patterns for Kids*, earned her teaching certification and bachelor's degree in English from the University of Texas of the Permian Basin in Odessa, TX. She has been teaching first grade for 13 years. Her last 8 years have been spent at Whitney Elementary School in Whitney, TX. Kristy recently won a Classroom Innovation Grant from First Choice Power. Her first-grade class also became a Model Classroom for the Reading Renaissance Accelerated Reader Program. Kristy lives near beautiful Lake Whitney, TX, with her husband and son.

For Product Safety Concerns and Information please contact our EU representative GPSR@taylorandfrancis.com Taylor & Francis Verlag GmbH, Kaufingerstraße 24, 80331 München, Germany

T - #0208 - 270225 - C0 - 276/219/3 - PB - 9781593633141 - Gloss Lamination